"SWEET LIKE HONEY,

KARMA IS A CAT,

PURRING IN MY LAP

'CAUSE IT LOVES ME."

-TAYLOR SWIFT
SONGWRITER
FELINE ENTHUSIAST

KARMA IS A CAT

IS A CAT

The True Stories of Meredith Grey, Olivia Benson, and Benjamin Button Swift

Written by Farrin Jacobs
Illustrated by Katty Huertas

TEN SPEED PRESS
California | New York

 CONTENTS

"YOU CAN'T SPELL *CATS* WITHOUT TS"

Meredith Grey, Olivia Benson, and Benjamin Button were unlikely siblings. It was the love of one woman that made them a family. That woman happens to be Taylor Swift, an international icon. She is an award-winning singer-songwriter, captivating performer, successful businessperson, supporter of human rights, and of course, most important, a lover of cats. The cats' story is also Taylor's story. And her story is one of a happy, talented child who grew up in a supportive family and who loved animals. She'd had cats when she was younger—Eliehsen and Indy. Little is known about these beloved feline Swift

predecessors (may they be living out the rest of their nine lives in a state of grace). They were family cats, though, different from the cat family Taylor went on to build.

Taylor has never been shy about proclaiming her love not just for her cats but for cats in general—and for this we adore her. Is it because they share so many qualities? Independent, observant, complicated, self-assured, attracted to shiny things . . . Taylor even attended cat school to prepare for a role in the movie version of *Cats*, a hit Broadway musical. By all accounts, she threw herself into the lessons and passed with flying colors—no surprise, really, because Taylor is very purr-ceptive.

It's possible that cats have been helping Taylor in small ways as she traveled her career path, and not simply by being cute and snuggly (or charming and standoffish, as

cats can, and have every right to, be). As she said in an early interview, it was a "'dad video' type of thing, with the cat chewing the neck of my [guitar] and stuff like that," that helped Taylor get her first manager. One of her singer-songwriter inspirations, Joni Mitchell, is also famously a "cat lady," as is Patti Smith, a singer-songwriter and poet whose name is featured in the song "The Tortured Poets Department." *Tapestry*, an album by another hero of Taylor's, Carole King, featured her tabby, Telemachus, prominently on the album cover.♥

In her almost two decades of being in the public eye, Taylor's fashion, musical genres, and guys have come and gone, but her love of cats has been constant. As she herself has pointed out, you can't spell *cats* without TS.

♥ Both Joni Mitchell and Patti Smith are visual artists as well. Like these creative geniuses, Taylor also paints and draws. She included some of her paintings in the magazine that was released alongside versions of her sixth album, *reputation*.

"Hanging out with my new roommate, Meredith"

Heart with number 2 at top.

Name: Doctor Meredith Grey Swift

Adopted: October 31, 2011

Breed: Scottish fold

Nickname: Mer

Top personality trait: Introversion

Likes/dislikes: Giving her mom side-eye / Having her picture taken

Taylor started her feline family on October 31, 2011, two days after National Cat Day, which is definitely a real holiday. She'd moved to an apartment of her own in Nashville, Tennessee, the previous year, and the time was right. She was on a short break during her *Speak Now* tour. "Guess what I'm doing tomorrow," she wrote in her journal. "Getting a kitten!" The US leg of the tour would be ending in less than a month, which meant plenty of time for snuggles, chin scratches, and purritos♥ at home. And then she'd get to spend both her birthday (December 13) and Christmas, her favorite holiday, with her new fuzzy daughter.

Possibly taking a page out of her parents' book—they named their only daughter after one of their favorite musicians, James Taylor—Taylor named her furry child Doctor Meredith Grey, "because she's grey." That's a big name for a little kitten. Taylor got it from one of her favorite TV shows, *Grey's Anatomy*.♡ The main character is named Meredith Grey, played by the actor Ellen Pompeo (who later appeared in Taylor's music video for "Bad Blood").

♥ A purrito is a cat wrapped like a burrito.

♡ *Grey's Anatomy* premiered in 2005, one year before Taylor began recording music professionally. The show even featured one of Taylor's songs ("White Horse") in an episode. This was a dream come true for her!

Doctor Meredith Grey Swift first appeared on social media on November 3, 2011. Taylor announced she'd gotten a new roommate and posted a picture of the cutest little fluffy kitten, who immediately purred her way into Swifties' hearts. Taylor is a mastermind when it comes to planting clues for her fans to find.♥ Maybe her Instagram post a few days earlier was a hint. "My day off shirt," she wrote, meaning the one she was wearing in the photo. "A gift from a super cool fan who knows that to me, relaxation = a shirt with a bunch of cats on it."

♥ these kinds of Clues are called easter eggs. tayloR started using them on her verY first album. certain letters in the Printed lyrics were emphasized to spell ouT a message. dedicated swIfties know to look for them in anything taylor Creates.

Meredith's early times as a Swift included hanging backstage while her mom performed for thousands of people a night during the final shows of the *Speak Now* tour, learning about the voting process for the Academy of Country Music Awards (her mom went on to win Entertainer of the Year), and just being generally adorable. Did she have a sense of how famous her mom was? It's hard to say, but it's safe to assume that she knew she was living the good life. And she got to travel with her mom a lot. Scottish folds are known to be cats who stay low—they're not big jumpers. Lucky for Meredith, it was easy to ride high in her mom's private jet.

Less than a year into her public life, Meredith was crowned the #1 Best Thing in Pop Culture by E! News. "Meredith was forged in the great Furnace of Cuteness," they announced. (Surely, they meant "*Fur*-nace," no?) Taylor worried that the attention was going to Meredith's pretty, round head. "She started out as a very friendly kitten," she said while she was promoting her album *1989*. "And then she became sort of an internet celebrity . . . and she changed a little. . . . She's always giving me the side glance. . . .

Like I don't matter anymore to her." (Considering Taylor couldn't promote her new album without everyone asking about her cat, Meredith might have had a point!)

Whether or not fame had truly changed her, Meredith basked in the glow of her star-studded life. Eventually she'd have to share the spotlight, though—she was going to become an older sister.

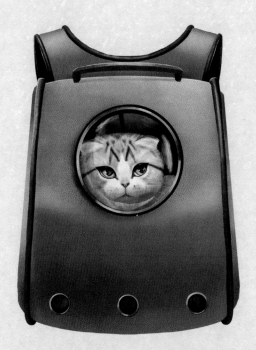

3

"MEET OLIVIA BENSON"

Name: Detective Olivia Benson Swift

Adopted: June 18, 2014

Breed: Scottish fold

Nickname: Dibbles

Top personality trait: Scrappiness

Likes/dislikes: Attention / Being called a nepo baby

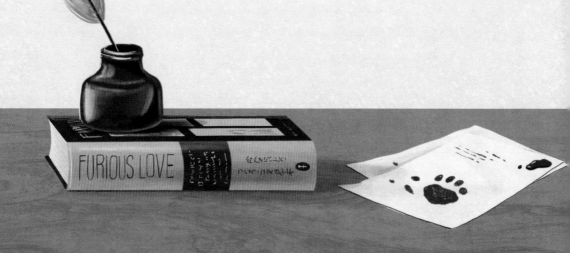

By 2014, Taylor had moved to New York City. Just as the tour for her latest album, *Red*, was ending, she decided it was time for her family to grow. "Meet Olivia Benson," she announced. She was developing a pattern—end of tour, new cat—and a theme for naming them: "strong women characters on my favorite TV shows." Meredith's new little sister's full name is Detective Olivia Benson, inspired by the

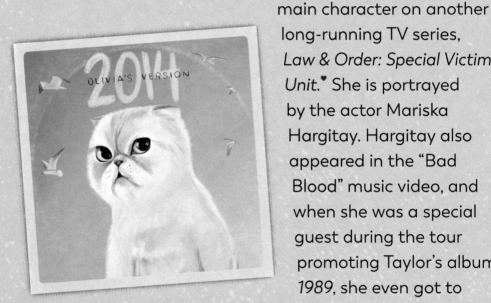

main character on another long-running TV series, *Law & Order: Special Victims Unit.*♥ She is portrayed by the actor Mariska Hargitay. Hargitay also appeared in the "Bad Blood" music video, and when she was a special guest during the tour promoting Taylor's album *1989*, she even got to

♥ *Law & Order: SVU* has been around even longer than *Grey's Anatomy*. The series premiered in 1999, when Taylor was only nine years old!

meet her feline namesake. In a Taylor-worthy twist, when Hargitay got a beautiful, blue-eyed Siamese kitten in 2023, she named her Karma, after one of Taylor's songs (the song that the title of this book comes from!).

The circumstances of Olivia's birth—as with most adopted kittens—are unknown. When Taylor first brought Olivia home, Meredith—characteristically and totally understandably—was not happy and let everyone know it. Taylor described their behavior as "like gladiators." But Mer was the princess of Kitty Town, wasn't she? She had to defend her territory. Who was this strange kitten everyone kept calling her sister? Where had she come from?

Eventually, Meredith accepted her new fate as the *older* instead of the *only*. But she did leave a nasty mark on her mother's leg only a few months later. Cats can be quite expressive in their own way.

They might be the same breed, but the sisters couldn't have been more different. Meredith has poise and a glare that could stop you in your tracks. Olivia . . . spends a lot of her time at the base of the stairs, belly up. "There are two kinds of cats," Taylor narrated in a video she posted of the ladies lounging at home: Meredith looking prim and decidedly catlike, and Olivia in full Dibbles mode, splayed on her back. The caption read, "In this house, there is no correct or incorrect way to relax."

One thing the sisters had in common—like Meredith before her, Olivia took to the spotlight. Olivia maybe even *took* the spotlight. Although Meredith was there for all the songwriting for *1989*, it was Olivia who was featured in the video for "Blank Space," one of the songs on the album. (Her mother held her in one hand while singing in bed—probably a daily occurrence, minus the wardrobe and camera crew.) And it was Olivia who appeared in the Keds campaign, her head resting on a "Sneaky Cat" sneaker. And an AT&T ad. And a Diet Coke commercial. (Was there any bad blood over this between the feline siblings? One wonders.)

Whether because of circumstances or the wisdom of her years, Meredith began to appear

on social media less often. Purr-haps their mom showing a home video called "Cat Fail" on the talk show *Ellen* had something to do with Meredith's changing attitude about her status as a public figure. The world saw Meredith fall and not land on her feet—paws-sibly the greatest humiliation a cat can suffer.

All in all, although the next few years were a roller coaster for their mom—a very public betrayal led her to live more privately for a while—for the ladies, life was pretty sweet.

About Scottish Fold Cats

All Scottish folds can be traced back to Susie, a 1960s barn cat from the Scottish countryside (a region called— are you ready for it?—*Tayside*). Yes, Susie is actual Mother!♥ Susie was the first cat known to have folded ears. Her mother's ears? Not folded. Her father's ears? Unknown. But her daughter's ears . . . were folded.

Other than their folded ears (which fold forward and down—but not all Scottish folds have ears that fold!), they generally have round faces and big, round eyes, a short nose, and a sweet disposition. People think they look like an owl in a cat suit. Their coats can be a variety of colors—one might be white and grey, while another is orange.

♥ Many of Taylor's fans jokingly refer to Taylor as Mother— because she is wise and sees all.

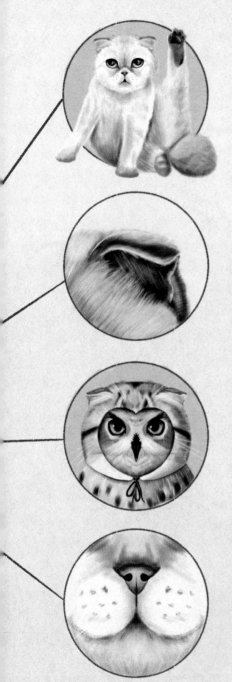

There is some controversy about Scottish fold cats. Because of it, Scottish folds should never be bred with another cat with folded ears. If so, the genetic mutation that causes that cute ear fold could lead to painful physical problems and a shortened lifespan. We know that Meredith and Olivia are very well taken care of, though. And Taylor's good friend Ed Sheeran also has a Scottish fold!

If you're at all familiar with Meredith and Olivia, you'll recognize some of these common traits:

★ Soft voice

★ Enjoys weird poses, like sitting up on hind legs and flopping on their back during naps

★ Not a loner, better with a friend (human or feline, or even canine!)

★ Playful

★ Adaptable

"AND THEN THERE WERE THREE"

Name: Benjamin Button Swift

Adopted: Early 2019

Breed: Ragdoll

Nickname: Benj

Top personality trait: Being adorable

Likes/dislikes: Starting fights with his big sister Olivia / Losing fights with his big sister Olivia

The internet is full of heartwarming pet adoption stories, but I think we can all agree that Benjamin Button's is fairy-tale-level heartwarming, or like something out of . . . a Taylor Swift song. It all happened the day the video for "ME!," the first single of Taylor's 2019 album, *Lover*, was filmed. The song is a duet with Brendon Urie from Panic! at the Disco (who apparently leaves exclamation points in his wake wherever he goes). The video begins with Taylor and Brendon playing a couple arguing. In an attempt to make up later in the video, Brendon offers Taylor some fancy gifts and she refuses them . . . until he tries a kitten. Everyone knows that *this* is the way to Taylor Swift's heart.

Before the scene was filmed, Taylor needed to meet the kitten who was about to be presented to her. And the moment he was in her arms, their eyes locked and he started purring. They were both wonderstruck. When Taylor found out that this little man didn't have a furever home—people in charge of bringing animals to a set often pick them from local shelters or rescue organizations—she hardly skipped a beat before deciding to bring him into the family, a little brother for Meredith and Olivia. The ladies were in the video, too, portraying Taylor and Brendon's "young daughters." Little did they know that the cat distribution system♥ was in effect and life was about to imitate art.

Taylor's meet-cute with Benjamin was captured on camera for the most adorable behind-the-scenes video everrrrr. "I know kittens are cute, but that kitten is special," Taylor says as she's telling someone that she's decided to adopt him. The day the music video was released, Taylor had an extra surprise for her fans: "And then there were three," she posted, along with a photo of her and sweet Benjamin showing the world his tummy. Then, as if to forever connect Benjamin to the *Lover* era, his likeness appears in other music videos from the album: his face is on the watch his mama wears in the opening of the "You Need to Calm Down" video, and a portrait of him

♥ The cat distribution system is what someone on TikTok called the phenomenon of a stray cat wandering into someone's life and becoming their cat. For example, you could go to work—maybe to film a music video—having no plans to adopt a kitten that day. Suddenly, an adorable kitten is placed in your arms, and . . . now you have a new cat!

is hanging on the wall of the house in the "Lover" video—during which Taylor watches the home movies featured in the "Lover" official lyric video. And of course Benjamin is also in those. Nothing Taylor does is accidental. Benjamin had arrived! For her new son, Taylor chose the name of the main character of a movie she loves. In *The Curious Case of Benjamin Button* (which was based on a short story by F. Scott Fitzgerald), the actor Brad Pitt plays Benjamin Button, who is born old and ages in reverse.

In 2014, when Taylor was pondering what makes a person a "cat lady," she decided the answer was three cats. "Three cats is a cat lady. Two cats is a party," friends told her. She had two at the time, Meredith and Olivia. Mer and Dibbles no doubt would've bristled at the idea that a person could have too many cats or that being a "cat lady" was something bad. Do they call a man with cats a "cat man"? Do they call a woman with three human children a "child lady"? They do not.

In 2021, one of Taylor's first posts on TikTok was the clip of her saying that three cats is a cat lady, and then a new video with her . . . three cats. Her caption: "*little did she know*." She was referring to herself in 2014. And when she was chosen as *Time* magazine's Person of the Year in 2023, she posed for the cover in a simple outfit of a leotard, black tights, and Benjamin Button draped over her shoulders. Those loud and purrrroud cat lady vibes were vibing now.

About Ragdoll Cats

Ragdolls are basically the Taylor Swift of cats: they've been named most popular breed by the Cat Fanciers' Association since 2018.

Purebred Ragdolls have blue eyes and are born with white fur, and their colors develop as they mature. They are one of several colorpoint breeds, cats whose body is lighter in color than their "points"—face, ears, paws, tail. Other colorpoint cats include Siamese and some Ragamuffins.

Ragdolls generally have long, fluffy fur; a long, fluffy tail; soft, triangular-shaped faces; wide-set, medium-size ears; and big, almond-shaped eyes. They come in a dizzying variety of patterns, and obviously Benjamin is Taylor's Version— seal bi-color. Seal is the color of his markings—a deep brown; and bi-color is because his face is two colors, with a white upside-down V cutting into the brown.

If you're at all familiar with Benjamin, you'll recognize some of these common Ragdoll traits:

★ Big and friendly and extremely chill.

★ Referred to as "puppy cats" because of their lack of boundaries and how they follow their humans around.

★ Gentle-giant vibe—the very definition of a lover not a fighter. Likely to sleep on their human (or . . . enjoy being held like a baby).

★ Not fully grown until about four (human) years old.

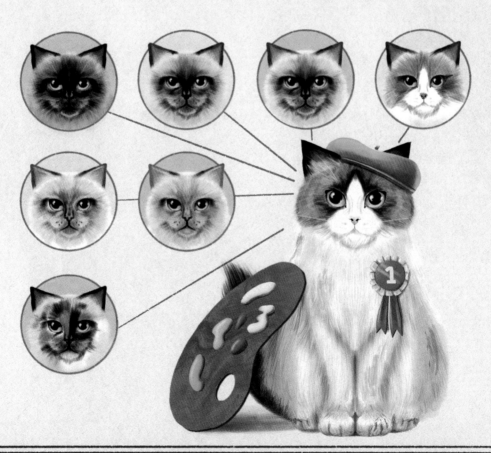

KITTY
COMMITTEE
STUDIO

"IT'S JUST SO MEOW"

By the time Benjamin purred his way into the Itty Bitty Pretty Kitty Committee, Meredith and Olivia were world travelers—wherever they found their litter box was home. Despite their status as global celebrities, their mom has made sure to give them as normal a life as possible. Her own close-knit family, which has helped her stay grounded, was a good model for this. From the outside, it might seem like an unusual life for cats, who are not known to be fans of regularly changing locations. Most have a routine and like to stick to it. (If you have a cat, you'll know this by,

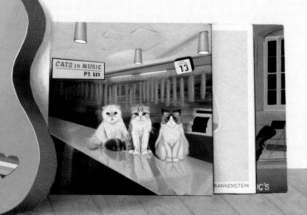

for example, how they will look at you with disdain if you oversleep and don't feed them on time. They have places to go, pen caps to chew!) To the Swift felines, however, this is simply life as they know it.

The ladies knew the drill: Mom writes and writes and sings and hums into that rectangle she's always taking pictures of them with. Then she waves her hand over the taut strings on that curved wooden thing, or sits at the big flat mountain and pounds out pretty noises from its black and ivory steps. Eventually she goes to a mysterious place called "the studio" and makes an album.♥ Next, she preps for tour, and then . . . they're off.

♥ Taylor's lyrics are often about her own life, but the only time she has specifically written about her cats was in the song "Gorgeous," off the *reputation* album: "Guess I'll just stumble on home to my cats."

Meredith, as the elder sibling, no doubt took the lead in showing Benj the ropes. She would've needed Olivia's help in getting him to understand that he couldn't always be carried around in his mom's arms, because she's a pretty busy lady. This time, the album release/tour cycle would be a little different, though. For *Lover*, Taylor had planned a shorter tour so she could spend more time with her own mom, who was having serious health issues. Even though her mom, Andrea, is partial to massive dogs, Taylor's furry children like their grandma. She'd been a good mom role model for Taylor—and who doesn't love Mama Swift?♥ She's the cat's pajamas.

♥ Taylor wrote about her mom and the comfort she finds in her love in "The Best Day" from *Fearless*. She also mentions her "excellent father" and her brother, Austin—"Inside and out he's better than I am." Family is so important to Taylor!

Suddenly, though, everything just stopped. There was a global pandemic. And their mom was home all the time. Which was great! But they didn't get to have that moment when they'd hear their mother come in the door and run to meet her so they could smell where she'd been and see whether she'd brought anything home for them. Sometimes their mother would interrupt a private sisters' moment, and while they knew it made her feel bad, it wasn't their fault she was born a human.

But they did get to witness what this "studio" thing was all about. Since their mom couldn't go to the studio, she brought the studio to her—and named it the Kitty Committee Studio. Turns out, it's just what she always does at home, but she does it with other people—over and over until it sounds how they want it to sound. The cats got to be in the room and witness the music magic as it was happening. Sometimes they chased one another across the bed and were shushed, but their mom said it was her favorite recording experience. In the immeowrtal words of their mom at the 2019 Teen Choice Awards, when she accepted the Icon Award that had been tailor-made for her and featured images of all three of her cats: *It's just so meow.*

TAYLOR'S ALBUMS AS CATS FROM *CATS*

While promoting *Lover*, Taylor identified all her albums as cats from the famous Broadway show and movie *Cats*. Here's what they'd look like.

VICTORIA
Taylor Swift

JEMIMA
FEARLESS

MR. MISTOFFELES
1989

GRIZABELLA
reputation

CATS

GUS
Speak Now

BOMBALURINA
RED

KARMA

MUNKUSTRAP
Lover

♥ Since she did this before she recorded *Midnights* and *The Tortured Poets Department*, those albums aren't included.

9
CALL IT WHAT YOU WANT

Being in the public eye means that along with the positive attention, you have to deal with strangers watching your every move, judging you, and even starting rumors about you. At one point, there was a rumor that the movie *Argylle* was based on a book Taylor wrote under a pen name! Why did people think this? Because the trailer featured a grey-and-white Scottish fold looking out the window of a backpack. . . . That wasn't the only rumor involving the famous felines. So let's clear up a few of the big ones about Meredith, Olivia, and Benjamin.

1. Meredith's Fashion Vendetta

It was May 2014, and the headlines were everywhere: "Taylor Swift's Cat Attacks Her Met Gala Custom Gown," "Taylor Swift in Met Gala Cat Attack," "Taylor Swift's Cat Meredith Nearly DESTROYED Her Met Ball Gown." (At least that last one named Meredith and didn't refer to her as just "cat"!) It all stemmed from a tweet her mother posted: "That moment when your cat casually walks up, then abruptly ATTACKS your custom satin Oscar de la Renta gown during your fitting for Met Ball."

Did Meredith really "ATTACK" the pink Oscar de la Renta gown? OK, yes. But did she "nearly DESTROY" it? Absolutely not. It was just a little fun. Who among us hasn't seen something soft and shiny and wanted to curl up in it? Trust that if Meredith had intended to destroy the dress, the dress would have been destroyed.

2. Cat About Town

A photo of Taylor carrying Olivia in her arms in New York City went viral in September 2014. Suddenly the headlines were everywhere—"Taylor Swift Explains Why She Carries Her Cat Around NYC!"—implying that Taylor spent her days strolling about the city with Olivia in her arms. "It was like a ten-foot walk from my door to the car!" Taylor clarified. One thing was certainly true about those pictures though: Olivia knew exactly where the cameras were and how to make sure they captured her best angles.

3. OLIVIA'S NET WORTH

When Cats.com claimed that Olivia is one of the richest pets in the world, a lot of social media gossip accounts and websites ran with the info. One writer called her a "nepo baby"! Just because she happens to be the feline daughter of Taylor Swift doesn't mean her success is due to nepotism. She is obviously talented. Like mother, like daughter not only in the talent category; both of their lives are catnip to the media. Olivia's net worth is nobody's business but her own.

4. Meredith's Disappearance

In 2017, Taylor had to take to social media to prove that Meredith was alive and well. "She takes it really personally," Taylor said of her firstborn, referring to all the rumors of her supposed demise. "It's hard for her. She now takes like seventeen naps a day." A happily napping Meredith filled the screen, her purr helping to put the rumors to rest. For a while at least . . .

5. Benjamin's Anti-heroic Traits

Forced to partake in the TS Anti-Hero Challenge, based on Taylor's song "Anti-Hero,"♥ where she reveals some of her less admirable qualities, Benjamin admitted that he allows his human to sleep in his bed. (Well, this is actually true.)

♥ Have you ever heard the phrase "I'm the problem, it's me"? This song is where it came from.

6. Meredith's Disappearance (Yes, Again)

In March 2020, Taylor posted an image of Meredith with the caption "For Meredith, self quarantining is a way of life. Be like Meredith." She was encouraging people to stay home during the pandemic, for the good of everyone. After the incident in 2017 and this post, you'd think the rumors about Meredith's whereabouts would stop. Nope.

Once again, Taylor had to provide proof of life. The storm had been brewing online for a while. "Where is Meredith?" people asked. She had not been seen on social media, and her fans were concerned. So in April 2021, Taylor announced that Meredith was alive and well, and that she simply doesn't like having her picture taken: "She's just a really private little cat."

Nobody can control what the media says about them— only how they react to it. As their wise mother once said, "I just kind of live a life, and I let all the gossip live somewhere else. If you go too far down the rabbit hole of what people think about you, it can change everything about who you are." And this was long before she wrote these lyrics for "You Need to Calm Down": "I've learned a lesson that stressin' and obsessin' 'bout somebody else is no fun / And snakes and stones never broke my bones." Mother knows best!

All the Cat Breeds TS Named on *The Tonight Show*

In 2022, Taylor was invited by New York University to receive an honorary doctorate in fine arts and speak to the graduating class. Now there would be two doctors in the family! In her speech, Taylor was quick to point out that she wasn't the type of doctor you call in an emergency, unless, she joked, "your emergency was that you needed a person who can name over fifty breeds of cats in one minute."

Soon after, Taylor was a guest on *The Tonight Show*, and the host, Jimmy Fallon, reminded her that she'd said this and challenged her to name as many cat breeds in thirty seconds as she could. Taylor is never one to back down from a challenge. The result was as impressive as you'd expect.

Scottish fold

Ragdoll

Ragamuffin

Maine coon

British shorthair

Exotic shorthair

American shorthair

Devon rex

Cornish rex

Sphinx cat

Abyssinian

Persian

Siberian

Burmese

Norwegian forest cat

Ocicat

Bengal

Bombay cat

Russian blue

Is there a British blue?
(There is, Taylor!)

Munchkin cat

Black cat ★

Calico cat ★

A cat that knocks
pens off desks ★

★Not official breeds, but definitely should be.

She Can Do It with a Broken Heart

People (who don't like or have never met a cat) have a lot of misconceptions about cats: they're aloof, they can't be trained, and they don't care about you. Nope, nope, and nope. Cats aren't just pretty faces. They can also be clever, silly, sweet, and . . . healing.

Merely petting a cat can be good for you and your stress level. With some cats, the side-eye energy is strong (looking at you, Meredith), but others, such as Ragdolls, are known to be so empathetic that they are recommended for use in felinotherapy—a real thing! Dogs aren't the only ones who can be therapy animals. Everyone should adopt a cat or three! While that sentiment will make some of those same people who have misconceptions about cats wonder whether a cat wrote this . . . Taylor herself has encouraged everyone and anyone to adopt cats. She has even donated money to animal shelters and rescue organizations.

A little known secret about cats is that they're loyal and protective of their humans. They just don't show it in the ways that other domestic animals do. While humans are the ones with opposable thumbs and therefore best suited to be caretakers, their cats are looking out for them in return.

Taylor has experienced a lot of heartbreak over the years—about boys, friends, her career, big life events, and small, everyday occurrences that feel big in the moment. And through it all, her cats have been a source of comfort. Pets in general can bring purpose and joy to one's life, but only cats have the magic of a purr, which has been known to help with stress. There have even been studies about how cats create sounds and vibrations at a frequency that literally heals. So a cat purring in your lap isn't only good karma; it's good medicine.

A note from legendary singer/songwriter Paul McCartney of the Beatles hangs on the wall in one of Taylor's homes.♥ It includes a favorite lyric from one of his songs: "Take these broken wings and learn to fly." It feels like advice Taylor has followed throughout her life and career. She has used heartbreak to create music that makes people feel seen and heard. Everyone knows that Taylor Swift *can* do anything with a broken heart,♡ but with Meredith, Olivia, and Benjamin she doesn't have to do it alone.

♥ She has four (as far as we know at this point) in the United States—in Los Angeles, Nashville, New York City, and Westerly, Rhode Island.

♡ One of the songs from her album *The Tortured Poets Department* is called "I Can Do It with a Broken Heart."

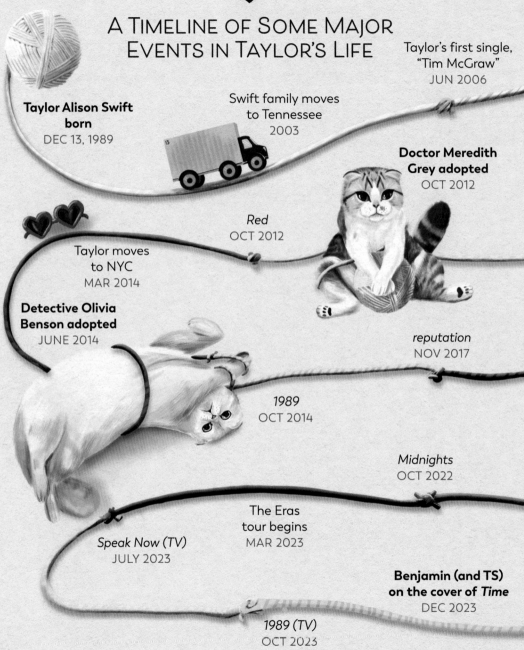

A Timeline of Some Major Events in Taylor's Life

Taylor Alison Swift born
DEC 13, 1989

Swift family moves to Tennessee
2003

Taylor's first single, "Tim McGraw"
JUN 2006

Doctor Meredith Grey adopted
OCT 2012

Red
OCT 2012

Taylor moves to NYC
MAR 2014

Detective Olivia Benson adopted
JUNE 2014

reputation
NOV 2017

1989
OCT 2014

Midnights
OCT 2022

The Eras tour begins
MAR 2023

Speak Now (TV)
JULY 2023

Benjamin (and TS) on the cover of *Time*
DEC 2023

1989 (TV)
OCT 2023

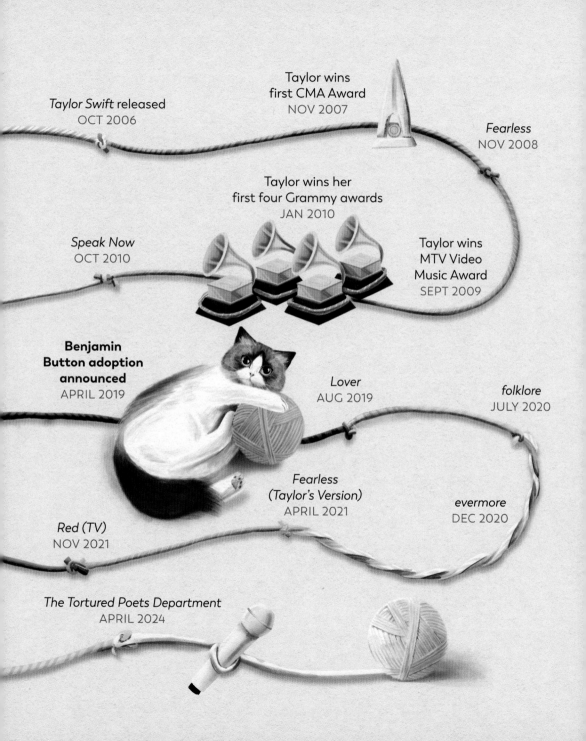

Taylor Swift released
OCT 2006

Taylor wins
first CMA Award
NOV 2007

Fearless
NOV 2008

Taylor wins her
first four Grammy awards
JAN 2010

Speak Now
OCT 2010

Taylor wins
MTV Video
Music Award
SEPT 2009

**Benjamin
Button adoption
announced**
APRIL 2019

Lover
AUG 2019

folklore
JULY 2020

Fearless
(Taylor's Version)
APRIL 2021

evermore
DEC 2020

Red (TV)
NOV 2021

The Tortured Poets Department
APRIL 2024

Adopt cats. And if you're lonely, adopt another one.
And just keep it up . . .

–TAYLOR SWIFT

Cats make everything better. I know it. You know it. But, in the United States alone, a million cats are surrendered by their humans to the more than fourteen thousand rescue organizations or shelters each year. In 2023, 4 million cats, including strays, went into shelters or rescues; only 2.6 million were adopted.

Not only has Taylor helped the cause by donating to shelters and rescues, but organizations have raised money and promoted adoptions in her honor. When the Eras tour hit Houston, Texas, the local humane society lowered adoption fees to thirteen dollars (Taylor's fave number, of course) for cats who had been in the shelter for thirty days or more.

If you're interested in bringing a furry friend into your family, you can adopt and provide a forever home. Or you could foster and help a kitty get out of a shelter temporarily. This not only helps the cat you're fostering, but it also frees up a space so another cat can be saved. There are many organizations you can turn to. Here are a few of our favorites:

❖ Best Friends Animal Society (national): www.bestfriends.org

❖ Petco Love (national): www.petcolove.org/adopt

❖ Brooklyn Cat Café (Brooklyn, NY): www.catcafebk.com

❖ City Dogs and City Kitties Rescue (Washington, DC): www.citydogsrescuedc.org

To my Best Girl, my Paula Perfect Face, sometimes Cujo,
always Gorgeous. I can't say anything to your face, 'cause
look at your face. I miss your big purr and soft fur.
I'm so glad I broke my kneecap because it led to you.

—FJ

To my husband, my family, and my furry friends,
who have inspired my art for years and even
posed for this book.

—KH

FARRIN JACOBS is an editor of bestselling and award-winning children's books, a writer, and a proud cat lady. A New Yorker at heart, she currently lives in Los Angeles.

KATTY HUERTAS is a multidisciplinary artist and illustrator born in Colombia and based in Washington, DC. She's collaborated with clients like Disney+, HBO Max, and Adobe, and her work has been shown in galleries across the country. Find her at kattyhuertas.com.

Penguin Random House values and supports copyright. Copyright fuels creativity, encourages diverse voices, promotes free speech, and creates a vibrant culture. Thank you for buying an authorized edition of this book and for complying with copyright laws by not reproducing, scanning, or distributing any part of it in any form without permission. You are supporting writers and allowing Penguin Random House to continue to publish books for every reader. Please note that no part of this book may be used or reproduced in any manner for the purpose of training artificial intelligence technologies or systems.

Published in the United States by Ten Speed Press, an imprint of the Crown Publishing Group, a division of Penguin Random House LLC, New York. TenSpeed.com

Ten Speed Press and the Ten Speed Press colophon are registered trademarks of Penguin Random House LLC.

Typefaces: Laura Worthington's Beloved, Latinotype's Boston, Igino Marini's IM Fell DW Pica

Library of Congress Cataloging-in-Publication Data is on file with the publisher.

Hardcover ISBN: 978-0-593-83758-0
eBook ISBN: 978-0-593-83759-7

Printed in the United States of America

Editor: Ginee Seo | Production editor: Serena Wang
Designer: Meggie Ramm | Art Director: Chloe Rawlins
Production manager: Philip Leung
Copyeditor: Heather Rodino | Fact Checker: Ashley Hannah Seo
Proofreaders: Vicki Fischer, Ann Gregory, Rita Madrigal
Publicist: Jana Branson | Marketer: Brianne Sperber

10 9 8 7 6 5 4 3 2 1

First Edition